*Cornerstones of Freedom*

# The NAMES Project

LARRY DANE BRIMNER

### CHILDREN'S PRESS®

A Division of Grolier Publishing

New York • London • Hong Kong • Sydney

Danbury, Connecticut

Visit Children's Press on the Internet at:
http://publishing.grolier.com

Library of Congress Cataloging-in-Publication Data

Brimner, Larry Dane.
    The names project / Larry Dane Brimner.
        p. cm.—(Cornerstones of freedom)
    Includes index.
    Summary: Describes the continually growing quilt that is being created
as a memorial to those who have died of AIDS and to draw attention to this
devastating disease.
    ISBN: 0-516-20999-X (lib. bdg.)    0-516-26517-2 (pbk.)
    1. NAMES Project Memorial AIDS Quilt—Juvenile literature.
2. AIDS (Disease)—United States—Juvenile literature. [1. NAMES Project
Memorial AIDS Quilt. 2. AIDS (Disease)] I. Title. II. Series.
RC607.A26B753    1999
362.1`969792`00973—dc21
                                                                98-49434
                                                                CIP
                                                                AC

Thousands of people walk among the panels of the NAMES Project AIDS Memorial Quilt. The mood is somber. The only sounds are muffled sobs and whispers.

A frail, gray-haired woman kneels at one panel and places a single red rose upon it. "My grandson," she says, her voice trembling. "He was such a good boy and now he's with the angels." He never forgot her birthday and returned to the family's Nebraska farm every summer to help with chores.

A middle-aged man kisses his fingertips and then touches them to a photograph sewn onto another panel. The little girl holding his hand says, "That's Mommy." Father and daughter had spent a year designing and sewing the panel to honor his wife and her mother.

*Family members look at some of the panels that make up the NAMES Project AIDS Memorial Quilt.*

There are more than forty thousand panels that make up the AIDS Memorial Quilt. Each panel represents at least one person who has died from an AIDS-related illness. Many panels represent the loss of more.

When Cleve Jones set out in 1985 to remember friends lost to the AIDS epidemic, he had no idea that the quilt would become both a symbol of government neglect and an international monument. His concerns were immediate. In November of that year, the number of AIDS deaths in San Francisco had reached one thousand. Afraid their names would be forgotten, Jones urged people to carry signs bearing names of the dead at a candlelight march on November 17.

At the end of the march, hundreds of San Franciscans paraded to the Old Federal Building. According to Jones, "People . . . taped the whole front facade of this grey stone building with these hand-lettered placards, with the names of San Franciscans who had died. It was a startling image." What Jones saw as he gazed at the names on the Old Federal Building was "a patchwork quilt," something that could be warm and comforting like the quilts of his childhood. Amazingly, one part of that "quilt" stood out. It was a fabric panel made by Michael Kensinger. Measuring 3 feet (1 meter) by 6 feet (2 m), the size of an adult human grave, it bore two names.

*Cleve Jones*

Jones, then thirty years old, was already a veteran of grassroots activism and no stranger to politics. He served as an aide to a California state assemblyman, was a cofounder of the San Francisco AIDS Foundation, and acted as a Sacramento lobbyist for the Quakers. His vision was to turn quilting, a traditional American craft, into a memorial for those lost to the AIDS epidemic. He also saw it as a tool for healing and action.

Almost a year after the candlelight march, the quilt began when Jones's best friend, Marvin Feldman, lost his battle with AIDS. With fabric and paint, Jones—who can't sew—created a panel in Feldman's honor. Like the panel made by Kensinger, this one measured 3 feet (1 m) by 6 feet (2 m).

Jones teamed up with Michael Smith and others to found the NAMES Project in June 1987. Operating from a storefront in San Francisco's Castro district, an area of the city especially impacted by AIDS, they called on people to create quilt panels in honor of friends and family members who had died. Their goal was to have a quilt ready to display on the Mall

*The panel that Cleve Jones made to honor Marvin Feldman began the project known as the AIDS Memorial Quilt.*

*Stacks of boxes containing panels for the AIDS quilt quickly filled the NAMES Project's headquarters.*

in Washington, D.C., in October 1987. The quilt was to be both a memorial and an illustration of the enormity of the AIDS crisis.

According to Smith, the quilt was also planned as a political protest. President Ronald Reagan had ignored the AIDS epidemic until May 1987, when he finally delivered a speech about it. But by then, thousands of lives had been lost to the disease. Smith and Jones hoped that the display of the quilt would prompt the president and other government leaders to take action in the battle against AIDS.

*Ronald Reagan*

The call for panels went out through a network of AIDS support groups, churches, and social-work organizations. To Jones's surprise, it was answered by people from all across the United States. Indeed, people from all over the world sent panels of friends and loved ones to be included in the quilt. At the storefront, volunteers gathered like an old-fashioned American quilting bee. They inspected each panel. They made those that required it stronger so they could withstand the trip to Washington, D.C. Then they sewed the panels together into squares that measured 12 feet (4 m) by 12 feet (4 m). There were eight panels to a square.

*Beneath completed portions of the quilt, NAMES Project volunteers use sewing machines to sew panels together.*

On October 11, 1987, the NAMES Project displayed the quilt for the first time on the National Mall in Washington, D.C. It included 1,920 individual panels and covered a space larger than a football field. The quilt was part of the activities at the National March on Washington for Lesbian and Gay Rights. That weekend it was visited by a half million people.

The quilt exists because of the AIDS epidemic. In 1981, gay men, or homosexuals, in many large American cities were

*When the quilt was displayed on the Mall in Washington, D.C., for the first time, it attracted thousands of visitors.*

being infected by a new and deadly disease. Some called it "the gay cancer" because it struck only gay men. Experts, however, named the new disease Acquired Immune Deficiency Syndrome (AIDS). The disease prevents the body from defending itself against infections. People can become infected with the virus that causes AIDS when they are exposed to the body fluids of people with the disease. This can happen during sexual intercourse or when blood is exchanged. That is why blood transfusions are now carefully monitored and people who inject illegal drugs are warned not to share needles. A woman who is infected with the virus can pass it to her baby.

9

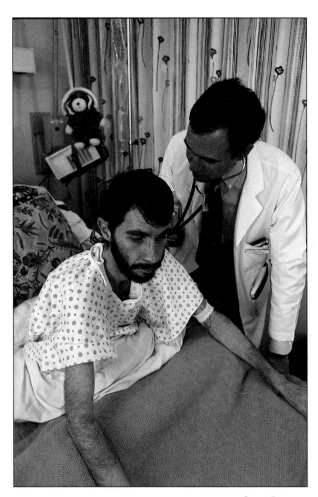

*At the time this photograph was taken in 1986, there was little doctors could do to treat patients suffering from the effects of AIDS.*

In the early 1980s, no one knew what caused AIDS. But it was clear that the number of people dying from the disease was increasing rapidly. Many in the gay community accused the government of being slow to react to the disease. They pointed to Legionnaires' disease as proof: When a handful of American Legion veterans was stricken by a mysterious type of pneumonia in 1976, the government had taken swift and immediate action to combat it. So far, the government had done little to battle AIDS. Critics charged that the president was to blame. He had been elected with the support of religious conservatives, who do not approve of homosexuals. Religious conservatives believe that homosexuality is a sin. Some of their leaders claimed that God sent AIDS to punish gays. The gay community believed that the government would have reacted more quickly had the disease struck a less controversial group of people. They accused the president of not caring.

As far as the public was concerned, AIDS was a "gay disease" (even though in Africa the disease

10

struck people of all ages and both genders). This made it easy to ignore because the majority of the people in the United States are heterosexual. They were not concerned with contracting the disease. The United States government at first offered only modest sums of money for research. Most religious organizations refused to extend a helping hand to those suffering from the disease. The news media had no interest in reporting on it.

AIDS, however, united people in the gay commu-

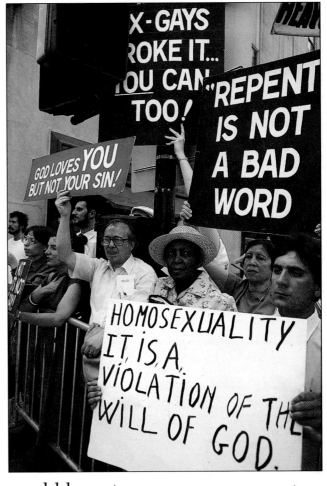

As AIDS gained attention, religious conservatives sometimes organized demonstrations to publicize their belief that homosexuality is offensive behavior.

nity. They realized that they would have to battle the disease themselves. They set up AIDS organizations, such as New York's Gay Men's Health Crisis, to raise money for research and to care for people living with the disease. They developed education programs to dispel the myths surrounding it. Ironically, when AIDS began to show up in women and children in the United States, many of them turned to the gay community for support.

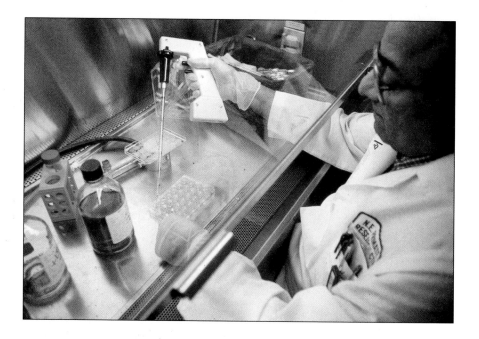

*Using funds provided by the federal government, a researcher works to develop a vaccine for AIDS.*

AIDS was a mystery illness. Rumors about it ran wild. Not knowing how it was transmitted, many people were fearful of anyone diagnosed with the disease. They were afraid that if they touched an AIDS patient, they might get the disease. They feared living or working in the same building that someone with AIDS shared. Because of religious beliefs and teachings, gay people had often been discriminated against. Sometimes they would lose their jobs or apartments when others discovered they were gay.

Now, AIDS caused the discrimination to worsen. Some hospitals and doctors even refused to treat AIDS patients. In October 1983, a Florida hospital sent an AIDS patient across the country rather than treat him. He died soon after arriving in San Francisco.

*Although well intentioned, some of the first informational pamphlets contained misleading information about AIDS.*

This became the first of many cases of AIDS patient "dumping," or refusing treatment.

Then in 1985, politicians, religious leaders, and reporters were forced to acknowledge AIDS. In part, this happened because Ryan White, a young hemophiliac, a person whose blood has trouble clotting, requested to attend public school in spite of being diagnosed with AIDS. Although by then experts believed that AIDS could not be transmitted by casual contact, parents of the other children protested. It was a case followed closely by the media. When Ryan, who died in 1987, was finally allowed to attend school, many of his classmates avoided him.

*This 1985 photo shows Ryan White in his room at his Indiana home.*

AIDS also struck Rock Hudson in 1985. Hudson was a Hollywood legend—a popular film and television actor and a longtime friend of President Reagan. Although diagnosed with AIDS a year and a half earlier, Hudson had tried to keep his diagnosis secret. His October death seemed to be the wake-up call that the United States needed. Not only could AIDS strike the poor and unknown, but it could also strike the rich and famous. Reports about AIDS suddenly filled every newspaper and magazine. Churches began to reach out to AIDS sufferers with support services of their own. But President Reagan still did not mention the topic for another two years. He even proposed a cut in AIDS research spending in his 1986 budget.

Groups formed of gay people and their heterosexual friends began protesting to raise the public's awareness about AIDS. They sang and chanted,

*Rock Hudson*

*By the mid-1980s, AIDS became the cover story for most of the country's major newsmagazines.*

LIFE

A Race To Save America's Great Movies

Koko (the Gorilla) Is Captivated by Kittens

That Fabulous Night: Teen Proms '85

July 1985/$2.50

NOW NO ONE IS SAFE FROM

AIDS

picketed and rallied. Gay people, who were con-
demned by some religions and sometimes denied
equal protection under the law, were demanding
respect, equality, and immediate action in the
battle against AIDS. Yet, in spite of increased
public awareness, many people remained
ignorant of AIDS facts. When three hemophiliac
boys in an Arcadia, Florida, family were diagnosed with AIDS, their house was firebombed.

*Parades such as this one in New York City in 1985 raised awareness about AIDS and other issues facing homosexuals.*

The defining act of 1987 was the National March on Washington for Lesbian and Gay Rights. Lesbians, or female homosexuals, and gays had gathered to protest their treatment and to demand equality under the law. In this atmosphere of anger and protest, the NAMES Project AIDS Memorial Quilt was spread out on the National Mall. It was a silent and solemn reminder of the AIDS toll and of people ignored. Amid soft crying, volunteers began slowly reciting the names of those represented by the quilt. It continued for three hours.

When Cleve Jones and the NAMES Project workers brought the quilt back to San Francisco, they were met by letters from people all over the United States who had seen the quilt on television or read about it in their local newspapers. Each requested the same thing: that the quilt be brought to their town. In

*Panels that make up the AIDS quilt fill the shelves in the NAMES Project's storefront. They didn't remain there long, however, as the public's desire to see the quilt grew quickly.*

*This June 1988 photograph shows the quilt on display in New York.*

*A Promise to Remember: The NAMES Project Book of Letters,* Jones reported, "So we bought a truck and set out on the first of what would be many tours, visiting the twenty largest U.S. cities. The Quilt grew as we traveled, for in every city we were presented with scores of new panels." The quilt tripled in size on the four-month tour and raised nearly $500,000 for AIDS service organizations.

By January 1988, the number of known AIDS cases in the United States had passed fifty thousand. The quilt continued to grow, adding panels with each passing day and with each city on the tour. By October, it contained 8,288 panels. Even so, this represented only a fraction of the total number of AIDS deaths.

The quilt returned to Washington, D.C., the next October where it was displayed on the Ellipse, the grassy oval in front of the White House. Once again, celebrities, politicians, family members, and friends read the names of those represented by the quilt, a rite that would be repeated at nearly every display. That same month, Congress passed a major AIDS bill that included $800 million in research funding. The quilt's goal to raise awareness was being realized.

There was still work to be done, however. Survivors of AIDS victims needed to mourn. Scores of people reported that making a panel for the quilt, though emotionally difficult, had helped them to remember, to grieve, and to

*Visitors on the Ellipse in late 1988 tour the display of the quilt.*

*Adults who brought children and students to view the quilt used the opportunity to teach them compassion for those afflicted with AIDS.*

let go of their loved ones. Panelmakers said that working with their hands was soothing and comforting. By gathering to share their grief, people were also learning and sharing the facts about AIDS, a disease still surrounded by myths. But the truth spread slowly and people continued to react to it out of ignorance and fear. In California, a proposal was introduced that would have required that AIDS sufferers be quarantined in special facilities. In Texas, a cafeteria worker at an elementary school was placed on paid leave because her son had died from AIDS. In both instances, the unfounded fear was that AIDS could be passed from person to person like the common cold.

In January 1989, the World Health Organization announced that there were 132,976 AIDS cases in 177 countries. AIDS clearly had become an international menace that knew no boundaries and for which there was no cure. So the quilt continued its work, going on tour again in the spring to visit nineteen additional cities in the United States and Canada. Raising $250,000 for AIDS service organizations, it ended the year with another October display on the Ellipse in Washington, D.C. That year it was nominated for a Nobel Peace Prize and a film, *Common Threads: Stories From the Quilt,* was recognized with an Academy Award.

However, the quilt was not without critics. Some people believed that confrontation was the only way to bring about change. The critics thought the quilt was too quiet and too passive. A group called the AIDS Coalition to Unleash Power (ACT UP), whose motto was "SILENCE = DEATH," was as vocal and active as the quilt was

*The filmmakers who produced* Common Threads: Stories From the Quilt, *with the Academy Awards they won in 1989*

quiet and passive. ACT UP members interrupted political speeches and blockaded roadways during rush hour. They backed up fourteen thousand cars on San Francisco's Golden Gate Bridge at the height of traffic. They passed out leaflets urging people to "Show . . . anger." They wanted the government and the public to feel as frustrated as the people who were living with AIDS and impatient for a cure.

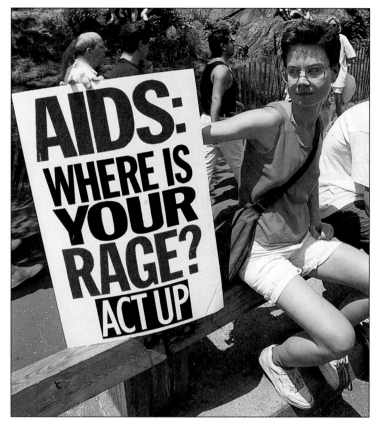

*A New York City demonstration by members of ACT UP*

Cleve Jones dismissed the critics, saying the quilt wasn't about anger, but about caring—for the living as well as the dead. "[W]hat [people] do is they come to the quilt, and they cry, and then they empty their pockets, and then they sign up and get to work." Since the quilt began touring, it had raised nearly $1 million. It had also heightened public awareness about AIDS and the slow progress that science was making in its efforts to find a cure. To the charge that the quilt was too quiet and passive, Jones responded, "Ha! Hardly."

*George Bush*

In spite of the quilt's successes, there were also defeats. George Bush had been elected president in November 1988, but many of his supporters were the same ones who had helped elect Ronald Reagan. In 1990, while saying that the disease "breaks my heart," he spoke against any additional funding for AIDS research and education because it was already receiving more funding than research into cancer and heart disease combined.

Yet it was clear that more education was needed. Many people still did not understand the disease. As a result, AIDS patients continued to be discriminated against. A municipal court judge in San Diego, California, ordered his courtroom disinfected after a man with AIDS appeared in it. Some AIDS patients were still denied hospital care when they became ill. A report by the National Commission on AIDS said that a "shocking number of medical practitioners refuse to treat people with AIDS." AIDS care facilities were also the target of frequent arson attempts. Equally tragic, by January 1991, AIDS had become the second leading cause of death among men between the ages of twenty-five and forty-four.

The worldwide picture wasn't any more encouraging. In October 1991, according to *Long Road to Freedom: The Advocate History of the Gay and Lesbian Movement,* "The World

Health Organization estimated that 1.5 million people, a third of whom were children, had developed full-blown AIDS." They suspected that nine million people were infected with HIV, the virus that causes AIDS.

So the quilt continued its work. By 1992, it contained panels from every state in the United States and twenty-eight foreign countries. Yet, even as science made slow progress into the mysteries of AIDS, others remained painfully unaware. A new drug called AZT seemed to be helping people with AIDS. But while on a visit to a New York hospital, Vice President Dan Quayle asked if AIDS patients there were taking DDT, a well-known poison. To draw attention to the global nature of the AIDS epidemic and to raise people's awareness, the quilt again returned to Washington, D.C. Displayed on the National Mall, the quilt covered more than 15 acres (6 hectares). By then, it was made up of twenty-six thousand individual panels.

*Portions of the quilt were sometimes taken to foreign countries. Here it is displayed in Yokohama, Japan.*

In 1993, the quilt gained new prominence. Newly elected president Bill Clinton invited members of the NAMES Project to march with the quilt in his inaugural parade. By then, however, it was far too large to appear in its entirety in a parade. Even so, more than two hundred volunteers carried sections of it.

When the quilt returned to Washington, D.C., in October 1996, it stretched from the Washington Monument to the Capitol, a

*Marchers in support of additional government money for AIDS research implored President Clinton to spend more money to combat the disease.*

*The quilt returned to the National Mall in October 1992. By then, it contained twenty-six thousand names.*

distance of more than 1 mile (about 2 kilometers). The display included forty thousand panels containing seventy thousand names. Many of the names were those of gay men, but a significant number of them belonged to women and children. Fifteen years after the disease had first been recognized, AIDS continued to be a menace. People were still dying. There was no cure in sight. Many still did not understand the awful impact of the AIDS epidemic.

By its very nature, a quilt is a fragile object. Public displays had been wearing on the quilt from the beginning. The tours kept a crew busy night and day mending and repairing. The quilt's last full display was in 1996. The NAMES Project doubts that it will be displayed again in its entirety. It has become too big. As of April 1999, the quilt was made up of more than forty-one thousand panels. It weighed 52 tons and spread out over twenty-five football fields. It contained almost eighty thousand names.

In spite of critics and opposition, and wear and tear, the NAMES Project continues its work with the quilt. Through the years, it has raised more than $2 million for AIDS service organizations. It has been seen by almost thirteen million visitors.

*The last display of the entire AIDS Memorial Quilt took place on the Mall on October 11–13, 1996.*

The panels speak their own language. Some are sad. Some are funny. Some are defiant. They are like pieces of the lives they represent. The panel for children's author Arnold Lobel—famous for his Frog and Toad characters—is appropriately decorated with frogs and toads. There are bits and pieces of people's lives, as well: Barbie dolls, old quilts, bubble-wrap, buttons, car keys, cowboy boots, flags, masks, rhinestones, and more. The panels also tell about the people who created them. The panel made by the Santa Clara/Santa Cruz Counties Council of Camp Fire Boys and Girls is filled with handprints that "symbolize that we are reaching out to help and love you."

*Schoolchildren in Santa Cruz, California, made the panel that honors children's author Arnold Lobel.*

Today, the quilt is also speaking to American teenagers. Ryan White's mother, Jeanne, wrote, "The Quilt gives my son, Ryan, a voice to help teach young people about . . . AIDS." Through the National High School Quilt Program any high school can receive sections of the quilt. Each school decides what AIDS prevention message is appropriate for its community and creates its own display.

*Ties and clothing worn by the AIDS victim make up his memorial panel.*

Andy Ilves, executive director of the NAMES Project Foundation, says that as long as AIDS is a menace and panels stream into the NAMES Project, the quilt will work to make people better informed. It will be a memorial to those lost to a global epidemic. It will be a symbol of hope. And always, its thread and glue will mend hearts.

*A woman mends the panel of a loved one at the quilt's last full display in 1996.*

# GLOSSARY

**arson** – deliberate burning of property with the intention of committing a crime

**defiant** – refusing to accept things the way they are

**discrimination** – prejudice or unjust behavior toward others based on differences in age, race, gender, or other factors

**facade** – the front of a building

**grassroots activism** – ordinary people organizing to create change

**inaugural** – the beginning of a president's term in office

**leaflet** – a folded, printed sheet of information that is usually distributed free

**lobbyist** – a person who tries to influence the voting of lawmakers

*panelmakers*

**panelmakers** – people who design and create the panels in the quilt

**placards** – signs or posters

**Quakers** – popular name for members of the Religious Society of Friends, founded in England in the 1600s

**quarantine** – keeping a person away from others in an effort to keep a disease from spreading

*placard*

**quilting bee** – gathering in which craftspeople, traditionally women, would sew together pieces of fabric to make a quilt

**symbolism** – when one thing stands for something else

**virus** – a tiny particle that can invade the body and cause disease

# TIMELINE

**1981** First cases of AIDS begin to appear

Cleve Jones leads candlelight march to **1985** San Francisco's Old Federal Building

**1987** *May:* President Reagan publicly mentions AIDS for the first time

The quilt visits twenty American cities

*October:* The quilt returns to **1988** Washington, D.C.; Congress passes AIDS research funding bill

*June:* Cleve Jones and Michael Smith found the NAMES Project

*October:* The quilt's first display in Washington, D.C.

**1989**

**1992** The quilt is displayed in Washington, D.C.

The quilt tours the United **1993** Marchers carry sections of the quilt in States and Canada, is President Clinton's inaugural parade displayed in Washington, D.C., and is nominated for Nobel Peace Prize; *Common Threads: Stories From the Quilt* wins **1996** Academy Award

Last full display of quilt on National Mall

Sections of the quilt continue to **1999** raise awareness in schools, libraries, and museums throughout the world

**INDEX** (*Boldface* page numbers indicate illustrations)

## PHOTO CREDITS

Photographs ©: Corbis-Bettmann: 8, 25, 30 top (Reuters), 14 top; Folio, Inc.: 1 (Robert Rathe), 18 (Lloyd Wolf); Gamma-Liaison, Inc.: 23 (Naoto Hosaka), 13 bottom (Hubbard), 12 (Peter Smith); George Bush Presidential Library: 22; Monkmeyer Press: 13 top (Van Etten), 21, 24, 30 bottom (Rogers), 2, 3, 5 (Vick); Names Project Foundation: 20, 31 bottom left (Ampas), 29 (Dale Baron), 7 top, 16 (Lance Henderson), 26 (Paul Margolies), 4, 31 top left; Photo Researchers: cover (Linda Bartlett), 28 (Leonard Lessin); Sygma: 7 bottom, 31 top right (Arnie Sachs); The AIDS Memorial Quilt Archives: 6, 27; The Image Works: 17 (P. Davidson), 19 (Nita Winter); Woodfin Camp & Associates: 9, 31 bottom right (Frank Fournier), 14 bottom (Bernard Gotfryd), 11, 15 (Alon Reininger), 10 (Jim Wilson).

## ABOUT THE AUTHOR

Larry Dane Brimner was born in St. Petersburg, Florida, and raised in Alaska and California. He attended San Diego State University, where he earned his B.A. in British literature and M.A. in writing. He has written on many topics for Children's Press. Mr. Brimner divides his time between San Diego and Rico, Colorado.